I Believe

Print ISBN 978-1-61626-838-1

eBook Editions:
Adobe Digital Edition (.epub) 978-1-62029-092-7
Kindle and MobiPocket Edition (.prc) 978-1-62029-093-4

Published by Barbour Publishing, Inc., P.O. Box 719, Uhrichsville, Ohio 44683, www.barbourbooks.com

Our mission is to publish and distribute inspirational products offering exceptional value and biblical encouragement to the masses.

Member of the
Evangelical Christian
Publishers Association

Printed in the United States of America.

I Believe

The Meaning of Christmas and the Baby Who Started It All

JoAnne Simmons

BARBOUR
PUBLISHING

$\mathcal{C}$ONTENTS

$\mathcal{I}$NTRODUCTION

Believe! It's a popular word for Christmas. You'll hear it in songs and stories, see it in decor and store windows, maybe even taste it in icing on a frosted holiday treat. But if you want to *feel* it, then its object must truly be worthy of believing in.

There are many traditions and values *believe* refers to at Christmastime—Santa Claus especially, if not literally the jolly, round man from the North Pole then figuratively for the generosity and magic he represents. Sometimes *believe* urges us to trust in the good in people, the good that's most evident during the season of giving. And sometimes *believe* just means hope—hope for things to get better because we all have hurts and hardships.

But to honestly say "I believe!"—to feel the faith those words express at Christmas—our object of belief must be the baby named Jesus. The baby who did come to make everything better. The baby who started it all.

This season, let Christmastime wrap you in a warm embrace, and in both the quiet moments and the bustling ones, may this book give you reason to pause in frequent prayer and say to the only One truly worthy, "Jesus, I believe."

THE STORY BEHIND THE STORY:
Ancient Prophecies Fulfilled

And it came to pass in those days, that there went out a decree from Caesar Augustus that all the world should be taxed. . . . And Joseph also went up from Galilee. . .unto the city of David, which is called Bethlehem. . .to be taxed with Mary his espoused wife, being great with child.

LUKE 2:1–5 KJV

So begins the best-known version of the Christmas story found in the Gospel of Luke, perhaps the best-known story of the entire Bible. Yet, what brought us to this point where the seemingly sad story of young, poor newlyweds having their first child in impoverished conditions has an entire holiday season—celebrated around the world—derived from and devoted to it? Could it be just a myth to base a celebration on? Just a fairy-tale excuse for a festive season to decorate, cook, shop, wrap, give, get, eat, drink, and be merry?

No, it's not just a story. It's *the* story! The story that, when studied in context of the prophecy it fulfills and the hope it provides, gives the purpose and meaning to life that every person is looking for.

So let's dig in a little. Why on earth was the birth of this poor baby Jesus—born in a barn!—so important? When we look at the story behind the story, the ancient prophecies that Jesus fulfilled, we see the importance. In the Old Testament, there are hundreds of prophecies about the coming Messiah, and all were fulfilled in Jesus Christ. After we take a closer look at a few of these, you'll have reason to say, "Jesus, I believe! I believe You are the promised Messiah who came and will come again!"

JESUS IS THE MESSIAH

Messiah is the Hebrew word for "anointed one," and Old Testament prophets had been promising the Jews for centuries that a Messiah was coming to rescue them from their oppressors. They longed for this Redeemer to come quickly, set up His new eternal kingdom, and rule with justice.

And finally the Messiah did come! Just not in the way most Jews had hoped for and expected. They were looking for a mighty King to arrive triumphantly, not a baby born in humble circumstances. But no matter how unexpected the method of His coming, we clearly see in the New Testament how Jesus fulfills the prophecies about the Messiah and comes as Savior not only to the Jews but to *all* people.

Jesus Said He Is God

The most important prediction about the Messiah in the Old Testament is that He would truly be God. That's a pretty big claim, and Jesus stated in various ways that He is the Messiah and He is God:

- Jesus declared Himself as the Messiah to the woman at the well: "The woman said, 'I know the Messiah is coming— the one who is called Christ. When he comes, he will explain everything to us.' Then Jesus told her, 'I Am the Messiah!'" (John 4:25–26 NLT).

- Jesus stated very clearly and simply, "I and my Father are one" (John 10:30 KJV).

- Jesus taught His disciples to pray in His name, saying: "In that day you will ask nothing of me. Truly, truly, I say to you, whatever you ask of the Father in my name, he will give it to you. Until now you have asked nothing in my name.

Ask, and you will receive, that your joy may be full" (John 16:23–24 ESV).

- Jesus prayed to the Father as one with Him: "Holy Father, protect them by the power of your name, the name you gave me, so that they may be one as we are one" (John 17:11 NIV).

- Jesus said that if we know Him, we know God: "If you really know me, you will know my Father as well. From now on, you do know him and have seen him" (John 14:7 NIV).

- Jesus said if we see Him, we see God: "Jesus saith unto him, Have I been so long time with you, and yet hast thou not known me, Philip? he that hath seen me hath seen the Father" (John 14:9 KJV).

- Jesus said if we receive Him, we receive God: "Whosoever shall receive one of such children in my name, receiveth

14

me: and whosoever shall receive me, receiveth not me, but him that sent me" (Mark 9:37 KJV).

- Jesus said if we believe Him, we believe God: "Jesus cried and said, He that believeth on me, believeth not on me, but on him that sent me" (John 12:44 KJV).

- Jesus said if we honor Him, we honor God: "That all men should honour the Son, even as they honour the Father. He that honoureth not the Son honoureth not the Father which hath sent him" (John 5:23 KJV).

- Jesus said if we hate Him, we hate God: "He that hateth me hateth my Father also" (John 15:23 KJV).

Not only did Jesus say that He is God, but He also said that He fulfilled all the prophecies about the Messiah. In the Gospel of Luke, after His resurrection, Jesus appeared to the two disciples on the road to Emmaus, spoke to them, "and beginning at Moses and all the prophets, he expounded unto them in all the scriptures the things concerning himself" (24:27 kjv).

When He appeared to the disciples in Jerusalem, He said, "These are the words which I spake unto you, while I was yet with you, that all things must be fulfilled, which were written in the law of Moses, and in the prophets, and in the psalms, concerning me" (Luke 24:44 kjv).

JESUS BEARS THE NAMES AND ATTRIBUTES OF GOD. . . .

Yahweh, is an Old Testament name for God derived from the Hebrew word for "I Am." In Exodus 3:14 (ESV), God reveals Himself to Moses in the burning bush and says, " 'I AM WHO I AM.' And he said, 'Say this to the people of Israel, "I AM has sent me to you".' "

One of the most powerful statements made by Jesus is in John 8:58 (ESV) when He says, "Truly, truly, I say to you, before Abraham was, I am." With this statement, He applies God's most holy name of "I Am" to Himself.

But anyone can say things about themselves without being honest, right? What if Jesus was just making extremely bold, but untrue, boasts? He wasn't; as proof, let's look at how the names and attributes of God in the Old Testament are the same as those of Jesus in the New Testament.

. . .*Immanuel*

The prophet Isaiah said clearly of the coming Messiah, "Therefore the Lord himself shall give you a sign; Behold, a virgin shall conceive, and bear a son, and shall call his name Immanuel" (Isaiah 7:14 kjv).

This is fulfilled in Matthew 1:22–23 (nlt): "All of this occurred to fulfill the Lord's message through his prophet: 'Look! The virgin will conceive a child! She will give birth to a son, and they will call him Immanuel, which means "God is with us." ' "

. . .*Son of God*

Psalm 2:7 (niv) says, "I will proclaim the Lord's decree: He said to me, 'You are my son; today I have become your father.' "

This prophecy is satisfied at the baptism of Jesus, when a voice from heaven said, "This is my beloved Son, in whom I am well pleased" (Matthew 3:17 kjv).

. . .*Mighty God*

Isaiah 9:6 (KJV) tells us about the coming Messiah: "For unto us a child is born, unto us a son is given: and the government shall be upon his shoulder: and his name shall be called Wonderful, Counsellor, The mighty God, The everlasting Father, The Prince of Peace."

New Testament accounts of Jesus fulfill the prophecies that the Messiah will be a Mighty God with a name above all names. Paul writes in Philippians 2:9–11(KJV), "Wherefore God also hath highly exalted him, and given him a name which is above every name: That at the name of Jesus every knee should bow, of things in heaven, and things in earth, and things under the earth; And that every tongue should confess that Jesus Christ is Lord, to the glory of God the Father."

. . .*Immutable*

Immutability is an attribute of God—He never changes! In Malachi 3:6 (NLT) God says, "I am the LORD, and I do not change. That is why you descendants of Jacob are not already destroyed."

Jesus' constant nature is evident in Hebrews 13:8 (NLT), which says, "Jesus Christ is the same yesterday, today, and forever."

. . .*Eternal*

God has always been and has no end! Psalm 90:2 (ESV) describes God this way: "Before the mountains were brought forth, or ever you had formed the earth and the world, from everlasting to everlasting you are God."

Jesus is also eternal. John 1:1–2 (ESV) says of Him, "In the beginning was the Word, and the Word was with God, and the Word was God. He was in the beginning with God." And in John 17:5 (ESV), Jesus prays to God, "And now, Father, glorify me in your own presence with the glory that I had with you before the world existed."

. . .*Omniscient*

God knows everything! One of the many Old Testament examples of God's omniscience is in Psalm 33:13–15 (NLT): "The LORD looks down from heaven and sees the whole human race. From his throne he observes all who live on the earth. He made their hearts, so he understands everything they do."

In the New Testament, we see evidence of Jesus' omniscience in places like John 16:30 (NLT), when Jesus' disciples said to Him, "Now we understand that you know everything, and there's no need to question you. From this we believe that you came from God."

. . .Omnipresent

God is everywhere—all the time! David wrote, "Where can I go from your Spirit? Where can I flee from your presence? If I go up to the heavens, you are there; if I make my bed in the depths, you are there. If I rise on the wings of the dawn, if I settle on the far side of the sea, even there your hand will guide me, your right hand will hold me fast" (Psalm 139:7–10 NIV).

Jesus shows us His omnipresence in the New Testament when He says, "Surely I am with you always, to the very end of the age" (Matthew 28:20 NIV) and "where two or three

gather in my name, there am I with them"
(Matthew 18:20 NIV).

. . .*Omnipotent*

God can do anything and has unlimited
power! In Genesis 18:14 (KJV) God asks
Abraham a rhetorical question: "Is any thing
too hard for the LORD?" Jeremiah praises God
for His power, "Ah Lord GOD! behold, thou
hast made the heaven and the earth by thy
great power and stretched out arm, and there is
nothing too hard for thee" (Jeremiah 32:17 KJV).

Jesus says He's omnipotent in Matthew
28:18 (KJV), "And Jesus came and spake unto
them, saying, All power is given unto me
in heaven and in earth." And He *shows* His
omnipotence through the many miracles He
performed, especially by raising the dead to life
(John 11:38–43; Luke 7:11–17) and through
His own resurrection (Matthew 28, Mark 16,
Luke 24, John 20).

JESUS' LINEAGE

Now that we've showed Jesus is God, let's jump back to Jesus' ancestors and take a quick look at how He fulfilled prophecy through His family tree.

In Genesis 3:15 (KJV), God is talking to the serpent and establishes that the Messiah will be a descendant of Eve, meaning that He would come through the seed of woman, not man: "And I will put enmity between thee and the woman, and between thy seed and her seed; it shall bruise thy head, and thou shalt bruise his heel."

Galatians 4:4 (KJV) fulfills this prophecy: "But when the fulness of the time was come, God sent forth his Son, made of a woman, made under the law."

This important prophecy and its fulfillment show how Jesus could be without sin (2 Corinthians 5:21)—because He was born through the seed of woman and so did not inherit the sin nature of Adam. Jesus is able to be our Savior from sin because He is the only One born *unable* to sin!

In various places, the Old Testament

tells us that the Messiah will be a descendant of Abraham (Genesis 12:3, 18:18), of Isaac (Genesis 17:19, 21:12), of Jacob (Genesis 28:14), of Judah (Genesis 49:10), and of King David (2 Samuel 7:12–13).

The lineage of Jesus given in Matthew 1:1–16 shows that these prophecies are fulfilled and verifies Jesus as a Jew and as a royal heir to the throne of David. Luke's Gospel also lists the lineage of Jesus for us in Luke 3:23–28.

JESUS' BIRTH. . .

Old Testament prophecies concerning the birth of the Messiah were fulfilled in detail in the New Testament when Jesus was born.

. . .to a Virgin

Isaiah 7:14 (KJV) says Jesus would be born miraculously to a virgin: "Therefore the Lord himself shall give you a sign; Behold, a virgin shall conceive, and bear a son, and shall call his name Immanuel."

This came to pass in Matthew 1:23–25 (KJV): "Behold, a virgin shall be with child, and shall bring forth a son, and they shall call his name Emmanuel, which being interpreted is, God with us. Then Joseph being raised from sleep did as the angel of the Lord had bidden him, and took unto him his wife: And knew her not till she had brought forth her firstborn son: and he called his name JESUS."

. . .in Bethlehem

Micah 5:2 (KJV) gives the location of Jesus' birth: "But thou, Bethlehem Ephratah, though thou be little among the thousands of Judah, yet out of thee shall he come forth unto me that is to be ruler in Israel; whose goings forth have been from of old, from everlasting."

In the Gospels of both Matthew and Luke, we learn that Jesus was in fact born in Bethlehem: "Now when Jesus was born in Bethlehem of Judaea in the days of Herod the king, behold, there came wise men from the east to Jerusalem" (Matthew 2:1 KJV), and "Joseph also went up from Galilee, out of the city of Nazareth, into Judaea, unto the city of David, which is called Bethlehem; (because he was of the house and lineage of David:) to be taxed with Mary his espoused wife, being great with child. And so it was, that, while they were there, the days were accomplished that she should be delivered. And she brought forth her firstborn son, and wrapped him in swaddling clothes, and laid him in a manger; because there was no room for them in the inn" (Luke 2:4–7 KJV).

. . . Worshipped by Kings and Wise Men

Psalm 72:10–11 (KJV) tells that kings
or wise men would travel to bring gifts and
worship Jesus: "The kings of Tarshish and of
the isles shall bring presents: the kings of Sheba
and Seba shall offer gifts. Yea, all kings shall fall
down before him: all nations shall serve him."

In Matthew 2:10–11 (KJV), the wise men
find and worship Jesus, offering Him the finest
gifts: "When they saw the star, they rejoiced
with exceeding great joy. And when they were
come into the house, they saw the young child
with Mary his mother, and fell down, and
worshipped him: and when they had opened
their treasures, they presented unto him gifts;
gold, and frankincense and myrrh."

Jesus Showed Us He Is God. . .

The Old Testament prophecies told not only who Jesus is and how and where He would be born, but also what He would do and what would be done to Him.

. . .by Performing Many Miracles

Isaiah 35:5–6 (NLT) is a prophecy about the miracles and healing Jesus would do during His time of ministry on earth: "And when he comes, he will open the eyes of the blind and unplug the ears of the deaf. The lame will leap like a deer, and those who cannot speak will sing for joy! Springs will gush forth in the wilderness, and streams will water the wasteland."

The New Testament Gospels describe many of Jesus' miracles—including changing water into wine (John 2:1–11), catching a large number of fish (John 21:4–11), calming the storm (Luke 8:22–25), walking on water (Matthew 14:22–33), feeding the five thousand (Matthew 14:16–21), casting out demons (Luke 4:33–37; Mark 5:1–13), healing the blind, lame, deaf, and sick (Matthew 9:20–22, 27–31; Mark 7:31–37; Luke 4:38–39; John 5:5–17, 9:1–41), and even raising people from the dead (John 11:1–44; Luke 7:11–17).

Who but the real Messiah could possibly do all these things?

. . .by Speaking in Parables

Psalm 78:1–2 (NIV) says, "My people, hear my teaching; listen to the words of my mouth. I will open my mouth with a parable; I will utter hidden things, things from of old."

And Jesus certainly did use stories to teach people: "Jesus spoke all these things to the crowd in parables; he did not say anything to them without using a parable" (Matthew 13:34 NIV).

I Believe

JESUS WAS BETRAYED

Several prophecies in the Old Testament give
specific details about Jesus' betrayal:

- Jesus would be betrayed by a friend.
  (Psalm 41:9, 55:12–24, fulfilled in
  Mark 14:18; Matthew 26:47–50)
- The price for the betrayal would be
  thirty pieces of silver. (Zechariah
  11:12–13, fulfilled in Matthew 26:14–
  15)
- The betrayal money would be used to
  buy a potter's field. (Zechariah 11:13,
  fulfilled in Matthew 27:6–10)

JESUS BORE OUR SIN AND JUSTIFIED US BEFORE GOD

One of the best-known prophecies of the
Old Testament encompasses Jesus' suffering
and sacrifice for our sins—His death and
resurrection and our justification before God if
we accept Him as Savior (Isaiah 53:4–12 NIV):

"Surely he took up our pain
  and bore our suffering,
yet we considered him punished by God,
  stricken by him, and afflicted.
But he was pierced for our transgressions,
  he was crushed for our iniquities;
the punishment that brought us peace was on
him,
  and by his wounds we are healed.
We all, like sheep, have gone astray,
  each of us has turned to our own way;
and the LORD has laid on him
  the iniquity of us all.
He was oppressed and afflicted,
  yet he did not open his mouth;
he was led like a lamb to the slaughter,
  and as a sheep before its shearers is silent,
  so he did not open his mouth.
By oppression and judgment he was taken away.
  Yet who of his generation protested?
For he was cut off from the land of the living;
  for the transgression of my people he was
  punished.
He was assigned a grave with the wicked,
  and with the rich in his death,
though he had done no violence,
  nor was any deceit in his mouth.

Yet it was the LORD's will to crush him and cause
him to suffer,
  and though the LORD makes his life an offering
  for sin,
he will see his offspring and prolong his days,
  and the will of the LORD will prosper in his
  hand.
After he has suffered,
  he will see the light of life and be satisfied;
by his knowledge my righteous servant will justify
many,
  and he will bear their iniquities.
Therefore I will give him a portion among the
great,
  and he will divide the spoils with the strong,
because he poured out his life unto death,
  and was numbered with the transgressors.
For he bore the sin of many,
  and made intercession for the transgressors."

All four of the Gospels attest to the completion
of this prophecy (Matthew 26–28; Mark 14–
16; Luke 22–24; John 18–21).

JESUS IS THE SAVIOR OF ALL PEOPLE

We've touched lightly on how Jesus fulfills the prophecies of the Messiah the Jewish people were longing for, but further study shows there are many other New Testament scriptures that prove His identity.

It's important to remember that Jesus is not Messiah to the Jews alone, but to the Gentiles, meaning all other people, as well.

In Genesis 22:18 (NIV) God tells Abraham, "And through your offspring all nations on earth will be blessed, because you have obeyed me."

And later Paul writes in Galatians 3:14 (NIV), "He redeemed us in order that the blessing given to Abraham might come to the Gentiles through Christ Jesus, so that by faith we might receive the promise of the Spirit."

JESUS WILL RETURN

The prophecies that Jesus hasn't yet fulfilled are those of His Second Coming—over a thousand Old Testament passages refer to it, and there are hundreds of references in the New Testament. (Zechariah 14:4; Acts 1:11; Matthew 24; Revelation 1:7; and Revelation 19 are just a few.)

But with all the evidence listed here that Jesus came as promised the first time—and again, we've just touched briefly on them!—we can be certain that Jesus will come again as the Bible says He will.

Jesus Himself told us many times that He would come again, perhaps most encouragingly in John 14:1–3 (NIV): "Do not let your hearts be troubled. You believe in God; believe also in me. My Father's house has many rooms; if that were not so, would I have told you that I am going there to prepare a place for you? And if I go and prepare a place for you, I will come back and take you to be with me that you also may be where I am."

So you see, there's much more to the story of the baby named Jesus who is celebrated at

Christmas. He's not just a myth or fairy-tale excuse for a season of celebration. The ancient prophecies that Jesus fulfilled and the hope He provides for eternity with God in heaven are the real reasons to celebrate Christmas! Jesus said, "I am the way, the truth, and the life. No one can come to the Father except through me" (John 14:6 NLT). And we can take Him at His Word!

Jesus, I believe in You! Your holy Word shows that You were promised to the Jews and to all people to come and save us from our sins. Your names, Your character, Your birth, Your life and ministry, Your death and resurrection—they all proclaim that You are God, and You are our Savior. I praise You for who You are and the prophecy You fulfilled. Jesus, I believe! I believe You are the promised Messiah who came and will come again!

The Nativity:
More Than a Tabletop Decoration

And she brought forth her firstborn son, and wrapped him in swaddling clothes, and laid him in a manger; because there was no room for them in the inn.

LUKE 2:7 KJV

You can find a Nativity scene in almost any format nowadays—blown in glass, carved in wood, molded into plastic toys so little hands can play without breaking. You can even buy a Nativity set of rubber ducks if you want. Nativity scenes come in all shapes and sizes, from tabletop sets to large lawn ornaments. Some churches even feature live Nativity scenes—arguably in the best ones, Mary holds a real baby, and there are actual donkeys and sheep to pet.

The word *nativity* means "the process or circumstances of being born," and while every new life is miraculous, it's a pretty common and ordinary event considering the number of babies born every day around the world. But the capitalized word *Nativity* refers to the circumstances of the birth of the baby Jesus, which is nothing short of a miracle. The almighty God humbled to the likeness of a human baby, born to a virgin in—of all places—a barn full of animals. Truly extraordinary. And when we explore the details of the Nativity and what they mean to us today, you'll find reason to say, "Jesus, I believe!

I believe Your Nativity shows how You relate to us. I believe You are Immanuel, God with us!"

Just an Ancient Scene from an Ancient Story?

The classic Nativity scene: the central focus is of course the baby Jesus in a manger, surrounded adoringly by Mary, Joseph, some shepherds, often wise men (their presence is a stretch of the story, however), and the livestock whose stable has been invaded by strangers and an infant. Over that stable a star might hover, maybe an angel. It's a scene that so many accept and display in their homes as a symbol of Christmas. An ancient scene from an ancient religious story that makes for a nice decoration but surely doesn't apply much to life today. . . does it?

Oh, but it does! The very nature of the Nativity shows how God was working to reconcile Himself to people then and now. The Nativity was God becoming *human*—born from a mother just like we are—God coming *to be with us*, God coming *to be our Savior*. And in each person, place, and circumstance of the Nativity, we find timeless ways to relate and lessons about God and our relationship with Him that certainly apply today.

And so it was, that, while they were there, the days were accomplished that she should be delivered. And she brought forth her firstborn son, and wrapped him in swaddling clothes, and laid him in a manger; because there was no room for them in the inn.

Luke 2:6–7 kiv

MARY

She was just a Jewish girl from Nazareth,
a young virgin named Mary, who was
engaged—betrothed actually, which was a legal
commitment at that time—to marry Joseph.
We don't know much else about her for sure,
but like most girls planning for a wedding, she
must have been excited about it and the new life
she would begin with her soon-to-be husband.
She could never have imagined the life God had
in store for her and Joseph though.

What was she thinking that moment
when a supernatural being, the angel Gabriel,
appeared to her and said, "Greetings, you who
are highly favored! The Lord is with you" (Luke
1:28 NIV)? Total shock must have taken over
for at least a few seconds, and questions like "Is
this for real?" must have been going through
her mind. The Bible says she was troubled, but
Gabriel comforted her fear then told her news
that must have sounded absolutely absurd. She
would give birth to the Son of God? His Name
would be Jesus? *What?*

Mary must have had a million questions,
but we only know for sure that she voiced one:

"How can this happen? I am a virgin." (Luke 1:34 NLT).

And he replied, "The Holy Spirit will come upon you, and the power of the Most High will overshadow you. So the baby to be born will be holy, and he will be called the Son of God" (Luke 1:35 NLT).

Mary could have told Gabriel he was crazy, and she was not buying a word he said. Or she could have believed but begged to back out somehow and not accept this position as the mother of the Son of God!

But God knew Mary. He knew she was the right girl for the job. She didn't scoff or complain at Gabriel's dramatic, life-changing news; she responded with obedience and praise to her Lord. She told Gabriel, "I am the Lord's servant. May everything you have said about me come true" (Luke 1:38 NLT). And later when visiting her friend Elizabeth, she gave praise to God with what is known as Mary's Song (Luke 1:46–55 NLT):

"Oh, how my soul praises the Lord.
How my spirit rejoices in God my Savior!
For he took notice of his lowly servant girl,
* and from now on all generations will call me*
* blessed.*
For the Mighty One is holy,
* and he has done great things for me.*
He shows mercy from generation to generation
* to all who fear him.*
His mighty arm has done tremendous things!
* He has scattered the proud and haughty ones.*
He has brought down princes from their thrones
* and exalted the humble.*
He has filled the hungry with good things
* and sent the rich away with empty hands.*
He has helped his servant Israel
* and remembered to be merciful.*
For he made this promise to our ancestors,
* to Abraham and his children forever."*

Though we don't know that much about
Mary, Luke tells us twice that she had found
favor with God (Luke 1:28, 30). Why was that?
What was so special about her that He chose
her from all the Jewish virgins to be the mother
of His Son, to fulfill the prophecy of Isaiah

7:14? We can't know the mind of God, but in Mary's response we gather a glimpse of why: she was willing to serve and be used by God; she was obedient to Him; and she obviously loved and trusted her Lord implicitly. That's clear in the way she readily accepts this huge, new, seemingly impossible task—and not only accepts it but praises God for it.

We can apply Mary's role in the Nativity to our lives today. God can use anyone—just like he used a simple young Jewish girl—to do great things for Him. The only requirements are willingness, obedience, and total trust and love. When God asks us to do *anything*, even something that seems utterly impossible in the world's eyes, we can respond with faith and praise like Mary, saying "I am the Lord's servant" (Luke 1:38 NLT).

Have you ever felt like you're nobody special—why would God possibly want to use you for anything good? Remember Mary.

JOSEPH

Joseph was a Jewish carpenter, trying to make a living, eager for Mary to be his wife. Following Jewish custom, Joseph would take her into his family's household to build their life together. What must he have been thinking when Mary came to him and shattered their dreams, telling him she was pregnant, but not with his child, with the Son of God? Shock for sure, but did he believe her or not? And then what? Humiliation, sadness, anger? Any number of feelings could have followed. Deep disappointment had to have set in when he made up his mind to divorce her, but he obviously cared for Mary because he "did not want to expose her to public disgrace" and "had in mind to divorce her quietly" (Matthew 1:19 NIV).

How many nights did he toss and turn, contemplating the divorce, missing Mary and all that could have been for them, before the angel of the Lord appeared to him? That angel appeared in a dream and said, "Joseph son of David, do not be afraid to take Mary home as your wife, because what is conceived in her is from the Holy

Spirit. She will give birth to a son, and you are to give him the name Jesus, because he will save his people from their sins" (Matthew 1:20–21 NIV).

Surely that dream gave Joseph relief, wonder, and anxiety all at once. Relief that Mary's words were true, and they could still wed. Wonder and joy at this calling to be the parents of the long-awaited Savior of all people. But anxiety over the logistics. How was this *ever* going to play out?

No matter what Joseph was feeling or thinking about all this, his actions are what matter. He obeyed God, despite the uncertainty. "When Joseph woke up, he did what the angel of the Lord had commanded him and took Mary home as his wife. But he did not consummate their marriage until she gave birth to a son. And he gave him the name Jesus" (Matthew 1:24–25 NIV). Three more times after this, Joseph obeyed when God directed him through a dream on how to care for his wife and adopted son (Matthew 2:13, 19, 22).

God might ask us to obey even when we don't *feel* like it, even when we can't see the way, even when we might face public disgrace for doing what is right. But God will provide the plan. He will show the path step-by-step—just like He did for Joseph.

Have you ever felt like you can't obey God because you'll be too embarrassed, or you can't see the whole picture? Remember Joseph.

Joseph. . .took Mary home as his wife. But he did not consummate their marriage until she gave birth to a son. And he gave him the name Jesus.

MATTHEW 1:24–25 NIV

THE SETTING

Joseph had a job and a home in Nazareth, so why on earth did his wife end up delivering the Son of God in a stable in Bethlehem seventy miles away from home? From the world's point of view, it was simply because of a government decree for a census that boiled down to collecting more taxes. "In those days Caesar Augustus issued a decree that a census should be taken of the entire Roman world . . . . And everyone went to their own town to register. So Joseph also went up from the town of Nazareth in Galilee to Judea, to Bethlehem the town of David, because he belonged to the house and line of David. He went there to register with Mary" (Luke 2:1–5 NIV).

But God was using these inconvenient circumstances for a greater purpose. He was fulfilling a prophecy, proving that He had sent the Messiah. As we learned in the last chapter, ancient prophecies said that the Messiah would be born in Bethlehem. "But thou, Bethlehem Ephratah, though thou be little among the thousands of Judah, yet out of thee shall he come forth unto me that is to be ruler in Israel;

whose goings forth have been from of old, from everlasting" (Micah 5:2 KJV).

And why a lowly stable, possibly a cave, that housed livestock? Yes, the town was crowded because of the census and all the inns were full. But surely the almighty God could have made a way for one single room to be available for His Son to be born in comfort. And yet He didn't: "And she brought forth her firstborn son, and wrapped him in swaddling clothes, and laid him in a manger; because there was no room for them in the inn" (Luke 2:7 KJV). But Mary, Joseph, and the baby Jesus were provided for all the same. The stable certainly wasn't luxurious, barely comfortable, but it provided everything they needed— shelter, a place to labor and rest, and a bed for the baby, albeit a manger.

God didn't bring His Son to us in extravagant luxury. Not even in middle-class comfort. No, He sent the Messiah to us in impoverished conditions to show us that Jesus came as the Savior for all people. He can identify even with those who have the least.

Even in the stressful, inconvenient

situations of our lives that seem at the time to have no other purpose than frustration, God can work to fulfill His purposes, to do His will. And that stable shows us that our Savior identifies with even the poorest of people, and He provides exactly what we need, when we need it.

Have you ever felt frustrated and discouraged by your inconvenient, stressful, possibly impoverished circumstances? Remember the setting of the Nativity.

But you, Bethlehem, in the land of Judah, are by no means least among the rulers of Judah; for out of you will come a ruler who will shepherd my people Israel.

Matthew 2:6 niv

THE SHEPHERDS

There wasn't a much harder or more humble job in Bible times than that of a shepherd. It was dirty, dangerous, exhausting, smelly, and lonely. Definitely not a prestigious or highly paid position. But on the night that Jesus was born, it was a group of shepherds who were invited first to visit the newborn Savior. You'd think at the birth of a King, the long-awaited Messiah, the first invited guests would be folks of high esteem. Yes, eventually Magi did come to visit Jesus, but not *first*. And they weren't personally invited by an angel of the Lord and witness to an entire host of angels illuminating the night sky with their presence and their praise. No, those honors were given to a group of common men, just doing their grueling jobs, living out in fields and tending to their sheep.

Imagine the looks on the shepherds' weary faces, when out of the dark of night an angel appeared saying, "Do not be afraid. I bring you good news that will cause great joy for all the people. Today in the town of David a Savior has been born to you; he is the Messiah, the Lord. This will be a sign to you: You will find a baby wrapped in cloths and lying in a manger" (Luke 2:10–12 NIV). And then, "Suddenly a great company of the heavenly host appeared with the angel, praising God and saying, 'Glory to God in the highest heaven, and on earth peace to those on whom his favor rests' " (Luke 2:13–14 NIV).

After the angels had returned to heaven, how long did it take the shepherds to gather their wits and say, "Let's go to Bethlehem and see this thing that has happened, which the Lord has told us about" (Luke 2:15 NIV)? Did they worry about their appearance or their odor? Did they hesitate and feel they were unfit to be in the presence of the Lord? Regardless, they followed the angel's directions and "hurried off and found Mary and Joseph, and the baby, who was lying in the manger. When they had seen him, they spread the word concerning what had been told them about this child, and all who heard it were amazed at what the shepherds said to them" (Luke 2:16–18 NIV).

God showed these simple men incredible favor the night that Jesus was born! And what a compassionate message God sent by inviting the most humble of people to the birth of His Son. The Messiah, who would later teach about caring for the "least of these" (Matthew 25:40) and liken Himself to a shepherd (John 10), displayed right from the start how important the poor and unlovely are to Him. He had come to be the Savior of all people, regardless of stature.

If you ever feel unworthy of Jesus, as if the tasks and sins of this world have made you too dirty to approach Him and accept Him, think about the shepherds of the Nativity.

And there were in the same country shepherds abiding in the field, keeping watch over their flock by night. And, lo, the angel of the Lord came upon them, and the glory of the Lord shone round about them: and they were sore afraid. And the angel said unto them, Fear not: for, behold, I bring you good tidings of great joy, which shall be to all people. For unto you is born this day in the city of David a Saviour, which is Christ the Lord.

LUKE 2:8–11 KJV

THE WISE MEN

On the night of Jesus' birth, not many people in the crowded town of Bethlehem realized the significance of the baby who'd just made His debut in a stable. It was a diverse guest list for sure—local, lowly shepherds and later wealthy, mysterious wise men from afar. These travelers came from the East to find Him. They arrived in Jerusalem, about five miles from Bethlehem, and asked, "Where is the one who has been born king of the Jews? We saw his star when it rose and have come to worship him" (Matthew 2:2 NIV). The wise men must have been surprised at the response they received. They had good intentions and were just hoping for directions, but they managed to cause an uproar. King Herod, and everyone else in Jerusalem, was disturbed. What were these strange VIPs talking about? Herod was king of the Jews!

So Herod called together all the Jewish religious leaders he could find, trying to figure these Magi out. And when the religious leaders reminded him of the prophecy in Micah 5:2 about a great ruler who would come out of

Bethlehem, Herod felt threatened. He didn't let
his fear show however. He cunningly convinced
the wise men to continue on their way and
report back immediately when they found the
new king so he could worship Him as well—
when actually he was planning to kill this new
king.

The wise men let the star lead until it
finally brought them to the home where Jesus
now lived. It was apparently a matter of days,
weeks, months, possibly even a year or two,
after His birth. "On coming to the house,
they saw the child with his mother Mary,
and they bowed down and worshiped him.
Then they opened their treasures and presented
him with gifts of gold, frankincense and
myrrh" (Matthew 2:11 NIV). Because of these
three gifts, we traditionally think there were
three wise men, but that's not for certain. No
matter how many there were, these men were
overjoyed to follow the star and considered it
an honor to find and worship the new King
Jesus. Why else would they travel so far, with
only a star and an old prophecy to guide them?

Very little is known about the mysterious

Magi. How long did they stay to visit young Jesus? Did they ask to hold Him or play with Him? Was Jesus old enough to talk to them? Did they hope He was pleased with their gifts?

On their way home, did they think the journey was worth it? They'd traveled so far, caused a controversy in Jerusalem, and now they'd been warned in a dream not to return to Herod (Matthew 2:12). They might have been traveling back to Persia or Arabia, possibly with fear motivating them to hurry. What would Herod do when he discovered they hadn't followed his orders? If Herod's furious decree to kill any child under two years old in Bethlehem is any indication (Matthew 2:16–18), we know he wouldn't have stopped short of killing the wise men either. Despite the weariness and worry that likely dogged them on the way home, surely the joy of following the star and finding the Savior sustained them.

Do you ever feel like it costs too much to keep seeking Jesus? As the wise men learned, following God's lead—even with the best intentions—is not always safe or comfortable or easy. And yet God provides direction, protection, and joy along the way. A star led the way as the wise men sought Jesus. His Word and His Holy Spirit guide us.

And when they were come into the house, they saw the young child with Mary his mother, and fell down, and worshipped him: and when they had opened their treasures, they presented unto him gifts; gold, and frankincense and myrrh.

MATTHEW 2:11 KJV

MOST IMPORTANTLY, JESUS

And saving the best for last—Jesus. The reason there's a capital *N* on this extra special *Nativity*. The miraculous, sinless baby wrapped in swaddling clothes and lying in a manger. As a baby and a child, what was He like? God in human form! Did He cry much? Sleep well? Have a favorite song or toy? As He grew, did He excel at everything? Run the fastest? Have favorite foods? To imagine God as a human baby, toddler, child, tween, and teen is absolutely head-spinning! And yet He did it. And while almighty God could have sent His Son in human form as some regal, superior ruler, He chose to send Him as a baby to common parents in common conditions, so that any and *every* human could find Him approachable. Even the name Jesus, which angels told both Mary and Joseph to name their holy child (Matthew 1:21; Luke 1:31), was common and relatable. Jesus is the Greek version of Joshua, meaning "God saves," and it was a popular name for boys at the time of the Nativity.

But this Jesus is Immanuel, God *with*

us. He came to know us and relate to us in every detail of our humanity, and He began His human journey just like we do, as a baby. Hebrews 2:17–18 (NLT) tells us, "It was necessary for him to be made in every respect like us, his brothers and sisters, so that he could be our merciful and faithful High Priest before God. Then he could offer a sacrifice that would take away the sins of the people. Since he himself has gone through suffering and testing, he is able to help us when we are being tested."

His purpose was to save us, to be our Messiah. Every detail of His miraculous birth, His life, His ministry, His death and resurrection provides a way for us to relate to God. He's the reason we're able to have a relationship with God, and apart from Jesus there's no way to God. "Be reconciled to God. God made him who had no sin to be sin for us, so that in him we might become the righteousness of God" (2 Corinthians 5:20–21 NIV).

We can still apply Jesus' teachings to our lives today; better yet, we can apply *Him* to our lives today. Have you ever felt like you need someone who truly understands you and can help you with your hurts, your fears, and your mistakes? Have you ever felt like you need a Savior? Reach out to Jesus.

For unto us a child is born, unto us a son is given: and the government shall be upon his shoulder: and his name shall be called Wonderful, Counsellor, The mighty God, The everlasting Father, The Prince of Peace.

Isaiah 9:6 KJV

WHAT TO DO WITH THE NATIVITY?

When you see Nativity scenes each Christmas
season, and as you decorate with your own
at home, reflect on each piece and what it
represents. The Nativity is so much more than
a tabletop decoration or lawn display. It's the
representation of hope for the world, our *only*
hope. It's God relating to us and providing a
way for us to relate to Him. Let God use the
people and circumstances of the Nativity to
remind you that He is with you, He loves you,
He understands you, He came once for you,
and He will be coming back for you. How will
you respond to Him?

Jesus, I believe You came as Your Word says You did. I believe in the people and places of Your birth story. Help me to learn lessons from the Nativity that deepen my faith and my relationship with You. Jesus, I believe! I believe Your Nativity shows how You relate to us. I believe You are Immanuel, God with us!

CELEBRATIONS FROM FAR AND WIDE:

Christmas Traditions from around the World

And the angel said unto them,
Fear not: for, behold, I bring you good
tidings of great joy, which shall be to all people.
LUKE 2:10 KJV

Santa Claus, Christmas trees, stockings, decorating cookies. . .those are just a few of the many popular traditions in the United States today. Have you ever thought to include piñatas, taffy, and fried chicken in your Christmas plans? In nations all over the world—sometimes in quieter celebrations because the holiday is not officially recognized, sometimes with bold festivities like fireworks—people celebrate Christmas. For many folks, it's all just for fun; they don't really understand or accept the significance of the Savior. But for others, the traditions and special activities of the holiday season are truly ways to rejoice in the hope and salvation Jesus offers every single one of us.

Yes, Jesus is the promised Messiah to the Jews. But like the angel said to the shepherds, the tidings of joy about Jesus were for *all* people, not just the Jews. And the unique and creative ways that God's people celebrate the Christmas season are fascinating!

As we look at a few of these traditions, may they remind you that while people of every culture are incredibly different, we're all equal in God's eyes, worthy to be saved and called His children! You'll have reason to say, "Jesus, I believe You are the Savior of *all* people."

ENGLAND

In England popular Christmas traditions include plum pudding, Christmas crackers, and listening to the Queen's speech.

Plum pudding is served as part of the big meal on Christmas Day. Covered with brandy and set on fire, it's brought to the dinner table with dramatic flair! A silver coin or charm is baked inside the pudding, and whoever finds it in his or her piece will supposedly have good luck in the coming year.

Paper-covered tubes called Christmas crackers are placed at each person's plate for the big Christmas dinner. They crack loudly when the end tabs are pulled, and out spill surprises such as paper hats to wear during dinner, small trinkets, and riddles to read aloud at the table.

After dinner families gather to hear the Queen's speech to the Nation and Commonwealth. This annual Christmas speech began in 1932 with King George V who, encouraged by Lord Reith, the general manager of the BBC, used the radio to address all his subjects around the world. King George VI and Queen Elizabeth II continued the tradition, and in 1957 the broadcast moved to television. Over the years, the format has changed from formal, live speeches, to prerecorded Christmas messages, to today's more relaxed broadcasts.

FRANCE

In France the most important Christmas decoration is the *crèche*, or Nativity scene. Nearly every home displays an elaborate crèche, which is the focus of the family's Christmas festivities. Little clay figures called *santons* (meaning "little saints") depict the people of the Nativity. Some families also put up and decorate a Christmas tree, but they're not widely popular, and the crèche is much more important.

On Christmas Eve families fast all day, attend Midnight Mass, and then return home or go to cafés that are open all night for *le reveillon*, a huge Christmas feast with a traditional menu that varies from region to region.

GERMANY

Outdoor Christmas markets in most cities are Germany's most famous Christmas tradition. Beautifully lit and decorated stalls offer all kinds of toys, gifts, decorations, treats, and beverages—anything shoppers need for Christmas—while choirs and brass bands provide festive music. The most popular Christmas market in Germany is the *Christkindlmarkt* in Nuremberg.

MEXICO

In Mexico, *las posadas* is a nine-day celebration that begins on December 16th. It represents the Holy Family's journey to Bethlehem and their search for a place to stay. In many neighborhoods, families will each schedule a night for the posada at their home. Children, often dressed as shepherds and angels, lead a processional of guests, including participants playing Mary and Joseph (or carrying statues of them), that travels throughout the neighborhood singing a song asking for shelter outside homes. When at last they find the home willing to invite them in, a party ensues with festive foods and often a piñata for the children. The last posada is on Christmas Eve and ends with Midnight Mass. When Mass is over, the church bells ring, fireworks go off, and many children receive gifts. Christmas Day in Mexico is a quieter time for church and family.

SPAIN

The Spanish Christmas season begins on December 8th with the Feast of the Immaculate Conception. In Seville, where the weather is warm, flowers bloom in December, and in the great cathedral there, costumed boys perform an ancient dance called *Los Seises* to honor the Virgin Mary, the patron saint of Spain.

Spanish children go from house to house at Christmastime, reciting verses or singing carols for treats and small toys. Tambourines, gourd rattles, castanets, and miniature guitars are sold in markets to liven up the singing and dancing in the streets. Large *nacimientos* or Nativities are set up in public places, and nearly every family has a small nacimiento in their home.

On Christmas Day relatives get together for feasting and exchanging gifts, and the children sing and dance around the nacimiento.

WALES

The Welsh people love music, and so *eisteddfodde* or "caroling" is an important Christmas tradition in Wales. Carols are sung in homes, outside, and in church where they are often accompanied by a harp. Every year a contest is held for writing new carols, and people gather in public squares to hear the one chosen as the carol of the year.

Taffy making is another popular Christmas tradition in Wales. Families make the chewy candy from brown sugar and butter on Christmas Eve. Historically it was a way to pass the time until *Plygain* (meaning "daybreak"), a special caroling service still held in many parts of Wales from 3:00 a.m. to 6:00 a.m. on Christmas morning.

We've barely scratched the surface on Christmas traditions around the world. You can find much more with a quick search online or a trip to the library or bookstore. What's truly fascinating is hearing from people who've experienced Christmas in a foreign country firsthand. . . .

AUSTRALIA

"Many Aussies eat seafood for Christmas dinner—prawns, fish, etc. My mother would often make Pavlova for dessert. It's an egg-white based recipe, and you put fruit on top (kiwi, passion fruit, etc.)."

SHARA LAWRENCE-WEISS,
native of Australia, now a wife, mother,
and business owner in the United States of America

BELIZE

"At Christmastime in Belize, it's fun to go into the city because there's always loud Christmas music playing in the streets. Belizeans usually paint their houses and put new floor coverings in for Christmas. They take time out of their day to go visit each other's homes the week before Christmas, sharing their delicious Creole light cake and black cake, which contains the essential secret ingredient of Belizean rum. The cake is usually served with orange Fanta or Coca-Cola. It's festive, in a tropical kind of way!"

JUDITH BEACHY,
Christian missionary to Belize

BRAZIL

"In Brazil we celebrate Christmas with a golden roasted turkey and a table groaning with traditional rice and beans, salad, farofa (manioc flour), and a stringy egg-yolk sweet called *fio de ovos*. Families get together for a big Christmas dinner. People make *rabanada*, which is like a glorified—and delicious—french toast with eggs, bread, and sweetened condensed milk. We don't have evergreen trees in the tropics, but people sometimes put up lights and decorations. Brazilians love holidays, so cities are shut down for several days at a time. It's hot and sunny.

"In Brazil the malls and shops are decorated with secular images of Christmas (lights, gifts, reindeer). Santa is a big draw. There are many Catholics and Protestants in Brazil, so those churches usually hold Christmas services as well."

JENNIFER ROGERS SPINOLA, resident of Brazil with her Brazilian husband for nearly eight years

CANADA

"What makes Christmas special in Canada is little things. Dessert for dinner is usually pie rather than pudding. After dinner there are a number of things we Canadians like to do. Like go for a walk no matter what the weather. Also the children (and those who don't consider themselves too old) play a game of fox and geese in the snow. And then we make a jigsaw puzzle. Christmas would not be complete without everyone gathered about the table trying to finish the puzzle before it's time for an evening snack. The other thing we do is listen to the Queen's speech. She's been reigning for 60 years, so we've listened to her as long as I can remember."

LINDA FORD,
Christian author living
in Alberta, Canada

CHINA

"In China Christmas is still not a largely celebrated holiday. It has become a mix of Chinese traditions with western elements. One tradition we have at the school we teach at is to have a Christmas club with many of our students. We invite them to our homes, eat lots of food, play games, decorate Christmas cookies, and share the Christmas story. Many of them have never heard it before and watching them listening intently as they hear of this little baby for the first time is incredible."

ELIZABETH B.,
English teacher in Beijing, China

COLOMBIA

"In Colombia Christmas is celebrated on the 24th of December. In the bigger cities everything is decorated in amazing lights, not just strung on trees but lit-up flowers and trains and fairies and much more! People also sell even more food and souvenirs on the streets, and it's like a huge ongoing festival. On the 24th people celebrate with family and friends, usually stopping in on many home parties consisting of delicious food, maybe some salsa dancing, and overall good fellowship."

DAWN HOFFMEYER,
Christian missionary with YWAM

GREECE

"The Christmas season begins in Greece on the morning of Christmas Eve with the sweet, clear notes of children's voices drifting over the land. Groups of children, bundled up against the cold, run from house to house caroling to the accompaniment of little silver triangles, which each clutch in their mittened hands. Hearing young children proclaiming the coming of the Lord's birth bright and early on the morning of Christmas Eve is a really special way to open the season. Then, on Christmas Day—the actual 'First Day of Christmas'—long before daybreak, church bells ring out in a melody of joy over the land calling the faithful to share in the glorious celebration of the birth of Christ. Before the sun has even dawned, people dress in their finest clothes and make their way to their neighborhood church. Churches around the country are bursting this day with people celebrating the birth of God incarnate!

"Children are off from school from Christmas Eve through the Feast of Epiphany (January 6th). The 'Twelve Days of Christmas'—extending from Christmas Day to the Eve of Epiphany—are a time of much joy with friends and family celebrating together. It is a very Christ-centered time."

ANN NICHOLS, housewife, author
(*The Faith of St. Nick: An Advent Devotional*,
Barbour Publishing) and resident of Greece

INDIA

"I actually remember as a kid in India walking to the bazaar with my family on Christmas Day for church and really noticing how oddly quiet things were, and wondering why no one else was celebrating with us! It was really different—everyone was just going about their business as usual, not knowing anything about the Christ who'd been born to save them/us that we were so eager to celebrate!

"We did our best as a church to celebrate though, and I do have fond memories of Christmas caroling together up and down the hillside several nights in a row around Christmastime. We'd be invited in for tea almost every place we stopped, and I loved singing along with the drums and guitars.

"I also remember being in several Christmas pageants (used for evangelism out in the villages during the Christmas season). I bet the sight of us little white kids dressed up as wise men and shepherds acting out the story of the Nativity with the adult church members was pretty interesting to the villagers watching!

"Looking back now on our time spent in

the villages, it is easy to picture Jesus born
in a stable in a village, too—simple and humble and poor—such a far cry from where we
are in the U.S. these days, especially around
the holidays, with our materialism and all.
Sometimes I miss it."

KRISTINE H.,
Christian missionary to India

ISRAEL

"Because Israel is a Jewish country, Christmas is not celebrated by the general public. We had a special Christmas story while we were there because of Messianic Jewish believers from our congregation who made it special for us. We had been in Israel for several months, and just before Christmas, my husband and I and two sons got a terrible case of the flu—it lasted for two weeks! We weren't even going to celebrate Christmas because we were so exhausted from being sick for so long. Our close friends invited us for dinner on Christmas Eve. Jewish believers generally do not celebrate Christmas, so when we walked in their house, we had one of the biggest surprises—they had completely decorated their home with Christmas decorations, a tree, and lights and had prepared a wonderful dinner for us. They had even wrapped gifts for us and put them under the tree. All of this was done completely for our benefit as they had never done any of that before. It was amazing, and we were so touched by the love of the Lord!"

LAURA G., Christian missionary to Israel

JAPAN

"In Japan Christmas is not an official holiday, so business goes on as usual on December 25th— schools, shops, the post office. Those who celebrate Christmas tend to be younger people, and the holiday is recognized (unofficially) as a time for couples and young love rather than families. People do buy Christmas cakes and Kentucky Fried Chicken around Christmas, with both traditions based loosely on European influences from the previous century. The Christian meaning of Christmas is not well-known, and it was not uncommon for me to meet children who thought the baby in the manger was baby Santa Claus.

"We Christians met together and celebrated with traditional dinners and prayers, and we often invited our friends to Christmas services at churches or homes. Japanese churches often have Christmas services with music, like Handel's *Messiah* in Japanese—something I'll never forget!"

JENNIFER ROGERS SPINOLA,
two-year missionary to Sapporo, Japan

KENYA, AFRICA

"Christmas in Kenya is a special opportunity to purchase new clothing, eat good food, and visit friends and family. Many of the Christmas traditions that Kenyans now follow started as a result of the influence from the foreigners who lived in the country. One example of a 'learned' tradition is the presence of a Christmas tree in the town square. The Kenyan tree, however, is decorated with streamers and balloons instead of the glittering balls and blown-glass ornaments that we use in the United States. Christ is recognized as the 'reason for the season' even in this far-off land where a white Christmas has never even been imagined!"

HEIDI OVERHOLT,
Christian Missionary to East Africa

LUXEMBOURG

"When I was in Luxembourg, I was there for St. Nicholas Day, which is celebrated on the 6th of December. It is actually a bigger holiday than Christmas. The kids leave out shoes, and St. Nicholas fills them with candy and toys and treats. My host family had a daughter with small children of her own. On St. Nicholas Day, the grandkids came over to the house, and their aunt dressed up as St. Nicholas and brought them presents. They were pretty excited, and although it wasn't like Christmas morning in the States, it still had the same feel."

LEAH VINCENT,
studying abroad in Luxembourg

MOZAMBIQUE

"For many, many years Mozambique was
a communist country, so Christmas isn't widely
celebrated where we live. Instead, people
celebrate what is called Family Day. It's a time
for families and friends to get together and eat
a special meal with chicken and cool drinks."

LISA HARRIS,
author and missionary in Africa

NEW ZEALAND

"Christmas in New Zealand happens in
summer since we are in the Southern
Hemisphere, so that means enjoying the hot
weather with a barbecue and visit to the beach!
A lot of families get together in the morning
to open presents together and have breakfast,
which often includes pancakes cooked on the
barbecue. That is usually followed up by a trip
to the beach to enjoy the sunshine and have
a swim in the ocean. For dinner we cook a
turkey on the barbecue and serve it along with
other favorites like roasted potatoes and a big

kiwi salad (which includes lettuce, carrots, onion, tomatoes, beetroot, and cheese). Our traditional dessert is Pavlova with whipped cream and fruit on top. People in New Zealand are quite laid back and often celebrate Christ's birth with a special midnight Christmas Eve service and spend time with family and relax on Christmas Day."

RACHEL McKEAN,
three-year resident of New Zealand

THE PHILIPPINES

"In the Philippines we celebrate Christmas with fireworks. Homes are decorated with Christmas lights—no pine trees. Everyone opens their homes and prepares lots of holiday foods like halo-halo, which is a dessert with exotic fruits, crushed ice, and coconut milk—yummy! It is a very loud and open celebration of the birth of Christ. It's like the 4th of July in December."

J. T. SPEELMAN, born in the
Philippines and raised in the
United States of America

POLAND

"On Christmas Eve in Poland, we arrived at our friends' house around 5:00 p.m. to coordinate when the first star appears in the sky. This is to represent the Christ Star. When the star appears, the festivities may begin. There were twenty-two of us gathered for the evening together. The grandmother then took a thin wafer called *Oplatek* and broke it in half, giving half to the next oldest person, and some words were spoken. This is such a nice tradition—each piece of the wafer is broken off and given to another member of the family, and then they wish each other a life filled with happiness, joy, health, and a blessed year. The wafer continues to be broken until everyone has had a piece. We were included in this, and it was so heartfelt and loving.

"Next we moved on to the food, and everyone sat at the table. I noticed that there was one empty spot, and I thought we were still waiting for one more person. I was wrong. In Polish tradition, an extra place is always set at the table for any unexpected guest. This is to represent Mary and Joseph with 'no room in

the inn.' At Polish tables there is always room
for the unexpected guest."

Leah Schneider Derewicz, Christian wife
and mom who loves to travel the world

SICILY, ITALY

"I was in Sicily in Italy over Christmas 2011.
We were in Syracuse just a few days before
Christmas, which coincided with the end
of the festivities celebrating the Feast of St.
Lucia. Her feast day is December 13th, but
the festivities last for a week. We got to see
the penitents come to the cathedral from the
city center in a long procession. They were all
carrying candles, and some were even barefoot!
Following the penitents came the big parade.
They paraded the statue of St. Lucia through
the old town to the cathedral, calling out
'Hail Lucia' and chanting. Sicily is a big citrus
region, and people were carrying large branches
with oranges on them instead of flowers or
palm leaves. There was a brass band, and they
even drove a ceremonial carriage through with

the relics, pulled by white horses. It looked like it was from the 1700s or so. There was a beautiful fireworks display at the end, which I got to watch from the roof of our hotel.

"Also in Sicily at Christmastime, there are carved or ceramic Nativity scenes everywhere. Every town has one, and every church has multiple ones. Some of the best were in Caltagirone, a ceramic-producing hub where we saw lots of terra-cotta créches."

LEAH VINCENT,
vacationed in Italy for Christmas 2011

SOUTH AFRICA

"Here, Christmas isn't about decorating trees, gifts, and Santa Claus, but instead spending time with family and friends. It's summertime, so many families travel for an extended holiday during this time. Christians often meet for a short service on Christmas morning and then spend the rest of the day getting together to *braii* (barbecue) and swim."

LISA HARRIS,
author and missionary in Africa

All around the world there are different cultures, different types of people, different ways to celebrate the Christmas season. Yet the Savior came to make us all *the same* through faith in Him. As the apostle Paul wrote in the book of Galatians, "For you are all children of God through faith in Christ Jesus. And all who have been united with Christ in baptism have put on Christ, like putting on new clothes. There is no longer Jew or Gentile, slave or free, male and female. For you are all one in Christ

Jesus. And now that you belong to Christ, you are the true children of Abraham. You are his heirs, and God's promise to Abraham belongs to you" (3:26–29 NLT).

Kala Christouyenna! (Greek), *Frohe Weihnachten!* (German), *Buon Natale!* (Italian), *Joyeux Noël!* (French), *Feliz Navidad!* (Spanish). There are so many ways to say "Merry Christmas!" So many unique languages of God's amazing people. And one day, the people of *every* language on earth will be proclaiming Jesus as Lord, because "God elevated him to the place of highest honor and gave him the name above all other names, that at the name of Jesus every knee should bow, in heaven and on earth and under the earth, and every tongue confess that Jesus Christ is Lord, to the glory of God the Father" (Philippians 2:9–11 NLT).

*Jesus, I believe all Your people are amazing!
There is so much diversity in the world, and
we can see it in all the fascinating ways people
celebrate the season of Your birth. The unique and
creative traditions among Your people show what
an amazing Creator You are. Thank You that
you came to save not just the Jews but everyone.
Jesus, I believe You are the Savior of all people.*

Sounds of the Season:
Stories behind Beloved Carols

And suddenly there was with the angel a multitude of the heavenly host praising God, and saying, Glory to God in the highest, and on earth peace, good will toward men.

LUKE 2:13–14 KJV

$\mathcal{W}$hat holiday other than Christmas has such a large selection of music—its own genre really—that most radio stations take days or even weeks off from their regular programming to play solely the sounds of the season? Yes, much of it is secular, with songs of holiday romance and wonderlands of snow, even Christmas donkeys and hippos! But surely you've noticed that the Christmas season is the only time of year when you'll hear Jesus proclaimed over and over from airwaves and speakers in nearly every public place. Not by preachers, but by musicians and singers to the tunes of our favorite religious Christmas carols. Many of the artists might not know or care much about the true meaning of the religious lyrics they're singing, but like the apostle Paul says in Philippians 1:18 (NIV), "What does it matter? The important thing is that in every way, whether from false motives or true, Christ is preached. And because of this I rejoice."

Carols, by definition, are songs of joy. Their melodies evoke emotions of joy, some quiet and fervent, others loud and triumphant. And each religious Christmas carol tells a bit of the story that brings the greatest joy to all people, the coming of Jesus as our Savior. Behind many Christmas carols there's also another great story, the tale of the circumstances or purpose behind its lyrics and tune. Let's look together at several Christmas carols, the meaning of their words, and the stories behind their composition. When we do, you'll have reason to say, "Jesus, I believe You give us real joy and are worthy of all our praise!"

JOY TO THE WORLD

Joy to the world, the Lord is come!
Let earth receive her King;
Let every heart prepare Him room,
And heaven and nature sing,
And heaven and nature sing,
And heaven, and heaven, and nature sing.

Joy to the earth, the Savior reigns!
Let men their songs employ;
While fields and floods, rocks, hills, and plains
Repeat the sounding joy,
Repeat the sounding joy,
Repeat, repeat, the sounding joy.

No more let sins and sorrows grow,
Nor thorns infest the ground;
He comes to make His blessings flow
Far as the curse is found,
Far as the curse is found,
Far as, far as, the curse is found.

He rules the world with truth and grace,
And makes the nations prove
The glories of His righteousness,

And wonders of His love,
And wonders of His love,
And wonders, wonders, of His love.

The writer of "Joy to the World," Isaac Watts, was born in 1674 at a time when his father was in prison for not conforming to the Church of England. Watts inherited his father's free-thinking, rebellious ways. He always wanted to change and improve rather than blindly accept the norm. This included standard church music, which Isaac found dull. Watts's father challenged him to create better church music and spurred his son to compose more than six hundred hymns.

While studying Psalm 98, Isaac Watts wrote "Joy to the World." It was originally sung to the tune of "Come Thou Fount of Every Blessing," but it wasn't embraced by many British Christians because they felt Watts was wrong to rewrite the Psalms. Until his death in 1748, however, Watts never gave up trying to improve church music, and his contributions and determination were hugely influential on other church-music composers.

The composer of the music of "Joy to the World" as we know it today was Lowell Mason, who, almost a century after Watts, was causing his own controversies in the church-music world. He'd been a student of George Frideric Handel, and in 1836, he wrote a new melody that he called "Antioch," which was inspired from parts of Handel's *Messiah*. It was three years before he found words for it—Watts's poem, "Joy to the World." This pairing of words and music created what is probably the most triumphant and jubilant song we love at Christmas.

O HOLY NIGHT

O holy night, the stars are brightly shining;
It is the night of the dear Savior's birth!
Long lay the world in sin and error pining,
Till He appeared and the soul felt its worth.
A thrill of hope, the weary soul rejoices,
For yonder breaks a new and glorious morn.
Fall on your knees, O hear the angel voices!
O night divine, O night when Christ was born!
O night, O holy night, O night divine!

Led by the light of faith serenely beaming,
With glowing hearts by His cradle we stand.
So led by light of a star sweetly gleaming,
Here came the wise men from Orient land.
The King of kings lay thus in lowly manger,
In all our trials born to be our Friend!
He knows our need—to our weakness is no
stranger.
Behold your King; before Him lowly bend!
Behold your King; before Him lowly bend!

Truly He taught us to love one another;
His law is love and His Gospel is peace.
Chains shall He break for the slave is our brother

And in His Name all oppression shall cease.
Sweet hymns of joy in grateful chorus raise we,
Let all within us praise His holy Name!
Christ is the Lord! O praise His name forever!
His pow'r and glory evermore proclaim!
His pow'r and glory evermore proclaim!

What a stirring song the beautiful "O Holy Night" is, but the story behind its original form is one marked with controversy.

The lyrics of "O Holy Night" were originally written in 1847 in French by Placide Cappeau de Roquemaure. He was a wine merchant from a small town in France, where he was also known for his poetry, so his parish priest asked him to write a poem for Christmas Mass. "*Cantique de Noël*" was the result. But he wasn't satisfied with it as a poem, so he asked his famous composer friend, Adolphe Adam, for help. Ironically Adam was Jewish—he was writing music for lyrics that praised a Savior and a holiday he did not accept or celebrate. Despite that, friendship motivated him, and he created a beautiful, original score to pair with Placide's poem.

Initially "Cantique de Noël" was widely accepted in churches in France—until Placide left the church to join the socialist movement and church leaders discovered that Adolphe Adam was Jewish. Then the French Catholic Church leaders denounced the song as unfit for church services. But the French people still continued to sing the beloved carol outside of church.

John Sullivan Dwight was an American minister who suffered from panic attacks during public speaking. Because of this, he became reclusive but used his writing talent to establish *Dwight's Journal of Music*. In 1855 he read "Cantique de Noël" during his research and fell in love. He kept the original meaning intact and translated it into the beautiful English text that we know today.

The touching melody and inspiring lyrics of "O Holy Night" focus on how one divine night changed the world forever—the Savior is born! He is our Friend; He is Love; He is Peace; *He is God*; and we should fall on our knees and praise Him forever with everything that is within us!

*Suddenly a great company of the heavenly host
appeared with the angel, praising God and saying,
"Glory to God in the highest heaven, and on earth
peace to those on whom his favor rests."*

LUKE 2:13–14 NIV

GO, TELL IT ON THE MOUNTAIN

Go, tell it on the mountain,
Over the hills and everywhere
Go, tell it on the mountain,
That Jesus Christ is born.

Can you imagine that chorus being sung
by dozens of slaves, voices lifted in soulful a
cappella praise to God, even as they labored
unjustly in humid southern cotton fields?
That's where it began. There's no one person
to give credit for the origin of this much-
loved Christmas carol—which began as
a spiritual sung by a group of oppressed
people, most of whom couldn't even read
or write. The influence of African American
slaves on Christian music is incredible, and
it speaks volumes—in light of their cruel
circumstances—proving that true joy comes
from knowing and worshipping Jesus as Savior.

Three generations of the Work family are
responsible for the full version of "Go, Tell It
on the Mountain." John Wesley Work Sr. was
an African American church choir director in
Nashville, Tennessee. After the Civil War, he

felt the new generation of black southerners needed to learn the importance of spirituality through the songs their ancestors had sung as slaves. His sons inherited his love of music and history and continued his work of collecting and creating new arrangements for old spirituals to keep them alive.

In the 1880s, John II and his brother, Frederick Work, studied "Go, Tell It on the Mountain." They wanted to keep the words and basic tune intact, but they rearranged them into a format that would fit choirs such as the Fisk Jubilee Singers, a world-traveling black musical group from Fisk College, where John II was a professor.

John Work III, a graduate of Juilliard, continued the family tradition of saving spirituals, often traveling great distances to find elderly former slaves who had sung them in the fields. During the Great Depression he studied "Go, Tell It on the Mountain" and reworked it once more into the arrangement and lyrics we know today, full of joy in the good news that "Jesus Christ is born."

GOD REST YE MERRY, GENTLEMEN

God rest ye merry, gentlemen,
*   let nothing you dismay,*
Remember Christ our Savior
*   was born on Christmas Day;*
To save us all from Satan's power
*   when we were gone astray.*

Refrain
O tidings of comfort and joy, comfort and joy;
O tidings of comfort and joy.

From God our heavenly Father
*   a blessed angel came;*
And unto certain shepherds
*   brought tidings of the same;*
How that in Bethlehem was born
*   the Son of God by name.*

"Fear not, then," said the angel
*   "Let nothing you afright*
This day is born a Savior of a pure Virgin bright,
To free all those who trust in Him
*   from Satan's power and might."*

The shepherds at those tidings
rejoiced much in mind,
And left their flocks a-feeding
in tempest, storm, and wind,
And went to Bethl'em straightaway
this blessèd Babe to find.

But when to Bethlehem they came
where our dear Savior lay,
They found Him in a manger
where oxen feed on hay;
His mother Mary kneeling
unto the Lord did pray.

Now to the Lord sing praises
all you within this place,
And with true love and brotherhood
each other now embrace;
This holy tide of Christmas all others doth deface.

God bless the ruler of this house,
and send him long to reign,
And many a merry Christmas
may live to see again;
Among your friends and kindred
that live both far and near—

That God send you a happy new year,
    happy new year,
And God send you a happy new year.

In fifteenth-century England, it must have
been tiresome for peasants to sing only somber,
mostly Latin songs in church. Because outside
of church, they created their own lively songs in
common language, which laid the foundation
for what we now know as Christmas carols.
"God Rest Ye Merry, Gentlemen" was a favorite
among the early Christmas folk songs. While
no one knows exactly who to credit for writing
it, it's obvious the writer knew the Gospel well
and understood the joy and importance of the
arrival of Jesus.

What's really interesting about the story
behind this carol is the original meaning of
the lyrics. What most people think of when
hearing or singing this song has nothing to
do with what it meant to its original writer.
Merry in the Middle Ages meant "great" and
"mighty." *Rest* meant "keep" or "make." And
there should technically be a comma placed
after the word *merry*. So when we sing "God

Rest Ye Merry, Gentlemen" today, what we really should be thinking is how the song means, "God make you mighty, gentlemen." And with the clear message of hope and joy that this song conveys, it can encourage all those who sing and hear it to take heart in the strength of our great and mighty God!

I HEARD THE BELLS ON CHRISTMAS DAY

I heard the bells on Christmas day
Their old familiar carols play,
And wild and sweet the words repeat
Of peace on earth, good will to men.

And thought how, as the day had come,
The belfries of all Christendom
Had rolled along the unbroken song
Of peace on earth, good will to men.

Till ringing, singing on its way
The world revolved from night to day,
A voice, a chime, a chant sublime
Of peace on earth, good will to men.

And in despair I bowed my head
"There is no peace on earth," I said,
"For hate is strong and mocks the song
Of peace on earth, good will to men."

Then pealed the bells more loud and deep:
"God is not dead, nor doth He sleep;
The wrong shall fail, the right prevail
With peace on earth, good will to men."

Still famous today as one of the greatest American poets, Henry Wadsworth Longfellow was a well-respected scholar, teacher, and writer in the 1800s. His life was full of tragedy though. He lost his first wife to illness in 1835, and in 1861 he lost his second wife, mother to their six children, in a fire. At that time, the Civil War—which Longfellow hated—was just beginning.

Despite a life full of worldly sorrow, Longfellow wrote a poem for Christmas in 1864 that still gives us hope today—"I Heard the Bells on Christmas Day." In 1872 an Englishman named John Baptiste Calkin composed the music for it.

Like Longfellow, we will experience tragedy, trial, even war in this world, but "God is not dead, nor doth He sleep. The wrong shall fail, the right prevail, with peace on earth good will to men."

O COME, O COME, EMMANUEL

O come, O come, Emmanuel,
And ransom captive Israel,
That mourns in lonely exile here
Until the Son of God appear.

Refrain
Rejoice! Rejoice!
Emmanuel shall come to thee, O Israel.

O come, Thou Rod of Jesse, free
Thine own from Satan's tyranny;
From depths of hell Thy people save,
And give them victory over the grave.

O come, Thou Day-spring, come and cheer
Our spirits by Thine advent here;
Disperse the gloomy clouds of night,
And death's dark shadows put to flight.

O come, Thou Key of David, come,
And open wide our heavenly home;
Make safe the way that leads on high,
And close the path to misery.
O come, Desire of nations, bind

In one the hearts of all mankind;
Bid Thou our sad divisions cease,
And be Thyself our King of Peace.

It's easy to imagine monks in the Dark Ages chanting those haunting words. Dating back to the ninth century, "O Come, O Come, Emmanuel" is likely the oldest Christmas carol still sung today. It was probably written by a priest or monk. In its original Latin text, it was sung or chanted for Vesper services during the Advent season. Most people who lived during the Dark Ages couldn't read and didn't have a Bible, and this song proclaimed the whole story of a Savior—the promised Messiah of the Old Testament.

John Mason Neale, a brilliant British pastor and scholar with a heart for the needy, made "O Come, O Come, Emmanuel" popular in the 1800s. He came across the original Latin chant during his studies and felt the text was important enough to be translated into English. He kept it paired with a fifteenth-century processional "Veni Emmanuel." It was first published in England in the 1850s and became popular in Europe and America.

"O Come, O Come, Emmanuel" may be a more subdued Christmas song, but the emotion evoked in believers by the chorus, "Rejoice! Rejoice! Emmanuel shall come to thee, O Israel" is nothing but exultant joy.

O LITTLE TOWN OF BETHLEHEM

O little town of Bethlehem,
*   how still we see thee lie!*
Above thy deep and dreamless sleep
*   the silent stars go by.*
Yet in thy dark streets shineth
*   the everlasting Light;*
The hopes and fears of all the years
*   are met in thee tonight.*

For Christ is born of Mary,
*   and gathered all above,*
While mortals sleep, the angels keep
*   their watch of wondering love.*
O morning stars together, proclaim the holy birth,
And praises sing to God the King,
*   and peace to men on earth!*

How silently, how silently,
*   the wondrous Gift is giv'n;*
So God imparts to human hearts
*   the blessings of His heav'n.*
No ear may hear His coming,
*   but in this world of sin,*
Where meek souls will receive Him still,
*   the dear Christ enters in.*

Where children pure and happy pray
to the blessed Child,
Where misery cries out to Thee,
Son of the mother mild;
Where charity stands watching
and faith holds wide the door,
The dark night wakes, the glory breaks,
and Christmas comes once more.

O holy Child of Bethlehem,
descend to us, we pray;
Cast out our sin, and enter in,
be born in us today.
We hear the Christmas angels
the great glad tidings tell;
O come to us, abide with us,
our Lord Emmanuel!

A preacher known as "The Prince of the Pulpit" in the mid-1800s wrote "O Little Town of Bethlehem." His real name was Phillips Brooks, and he is now recognized as one of the most outstanding preachers of the nineteenth century.

In December 1865, Brooks was on

a sabbatical tour of the Middle East. On Christmas Eve in Jerusalem, he felt the urge to get away from the crowds in the city, so he borrowed a horse and set out into the countryside. At dusk he rode into the village of Bethlehem and was awed and inspired to be in the place of Jesus' birth, on streets practically unchanged since that time.

For a long time after that trip, Brooks couldn't find the right words to describe the spiritual experience he'd had in Bethlehem. But as he prepared for the holiday season of 1868, he was able to write adequate words in the form of a poem. He shared it with a friend and organist, Lewis Redner, who also struggled to compose the right music to accompany it. It wasn't until he gave up and went to sleep on Christmas Eve that the music came to him. He woke up, and calling it a gift from heaven, he wrote the beloved music of "O Little Town of Bethlehem."

SILENT NIGHT

Silent night, holy night,
All is calm, all is bright
Round yon virgin mother and Child.
Holy Infant, so tender and mild,
Sleep in heavenly peace,
Sleep in heavenly peace.

Silent night, holy night,
Shepherds quake at the sight;
Glories stream from heaven afar,
Heavenly hosts sing Alleluia!
Christ the Savior is born,
Christ the Savior is born!

Silent night, holy night,
Son of God, love's pure light;
Radiant beams from Thy holy face
With the dawn of redeeming grace,
Jesus, Lord, at Thy birth,
Jesus, Lord, at Thy birth.

Silent night, holy night
Wondrous star, lend thy light;
With the angels let us sing,

Alleluia to our King;
Christ the Savior is born,
Christ the Savior is born!

"Silent Night" was born out of necessity in
1818 when a church organ in Oberndorf in
the Tyrol region of Austria wouldn't play, and
the parish priest, Joseph Mohr, was frantically
determined that Christmas Eve Mass would
still include music.

Mohr dug out a Christmas poem he'd
written previously called "*Stille Nacht! Heilige*
Nacht!" and took it to his friend Franz Gruber,
the village schoolteacher and church organist.
With only hours until Christmas Eve services
would begin, Mohr asked Gruber to write
music to fit the poem that could be played on a
guitar since the organ was not working. Gruber
accepted the challenge and composed a simple,
sweet melody for the song just in time. That
night Mohr and Gruber sang together with
the strum of the guitar and introduced their
congregation to the new Christmas song.

Days later, organ builder Karl Mauracher
repaired the organ and was impressed when

he heard the new carol and learned the story of urgency behind it. Over the next few years he promoted "Stille Nacht!" and introduced it to many churches and towns in the Tyrol. It continued to gain popularity and was spread to more areas of Europe by traveling folk singers.

In 1839 the Austrian folk group the Rainers traveled to New York and sang "Stille Nacht!" in English for a crowd at Trinity Church. By the Civil War it had become America's favorite Christmas carol and is still one of the most-recorded songs in history—a song that embraces the sacredness of the night Jesus was born, the joy that "Christ the Savior is born, Christ the Savior is born!"

HARK THE HERALD ANGELS SING

Hark! The herald angels sing,
"Glory to the newborn King;
Peace on earth, and mercy mild,
God and sinners reconciled!"
Joyful, all ye nations rise,
Join the triumph of the skies;
With th'angelic host proclaim,
"Christ is born in Bethlehem!"

Hark! the herald angels sing,
"Glory to the newborn King!"

The story of "Hark the Herald Angels Sing" is a story of conflict, because George Whitefield changed, without permission, the original words of Charles Wesley's hymn "Hark! How all the Welkin Rings." (*Welkin* means "the heavens.") Here's a portion of the original words by Charles Wesley:

Hark, how all the welkin rings,
"Glory to the King of kings;
Peace on earth, and mercy mild,
God and sinners reconciled!"

Joyful, all ye nations, rise,
Join the triumph of the skies;
Universal nature say,
"Christ the Lord is born to-day!"

Because of Whitefield's lyrics, even though angels don't actually *sing* about Jesus' arrival anywhere in the Bible, singing angels are a common misconception that are embraced in Christmas sermons, songs, stories, and art!

The angels might not have sung, but we do. And when we sing, our intent should be the same as the praise spoken joyfully by those angels—to give glory to God for sending us the Savior!

*Jesus, for all that You are and all that You do,
I believe we have every reason to worship You.
The peace and comfort You give—in the good
times and the bad—inspire Your people to
make music and sing to You, especially at
Christmastime. Jesus, I believe You give us real
joy and are worthy of all our praise!*

Holiday Festivities:

The Meaning and History of Christmas Traditions

*But Mary kept all these things,
and pondered them in her heart.*
LUKE 2:19 KJV

So much happened the night of the Jesus' birth. The new mother Mary was surely overwhelmed with all kinds of emotions, exhaustion amplifying them all. Wonder and awe probably topped her list of feelings. Had all this really happened? Were those nine months of pregnancy and the journey to Bethlehem real? Why did they have to end up in a stable of all places? Did she truly deliver the Son of God? Was it her Savior she cuddled close to her? And then shepherds came to visit her baby, so excited about what an angel had told them about her baby. There was so much to think over! So "Mary kept all these things, and pondered them in her heart."

The first couple chapters of the Gospels of Matthew and Luke tell just a small summary of the Nativity. We have so much to guess about, so much to question. And over the centuries, speculation and attempts to remember and retell it have led to enduring Christmas traditions that we observe and enjoy today. Other famous traditions have also evolved, not necessarily in honor of Jesus and His birth, but often out of the desire to show compassion and generosity during this special holiday season. By now, though, many of them are observed without much thought to the significance or history behind them. But to truly appreciate them, they need to be pondered just like Mary pondered the events of Jesus' birth. As we look at the deeper meaning and the history behind several of today's favorite Christmas traditions, you'll have reason to say, "Jesus, I believe we should honor You in everything we do!"

DECEMBER 25

Unfortunately we have no birth certificate telling us the exact date Jesus entered the world. So who came up with it? Is it even remotely accurate? Maybe, maybe not. But there is a story behind it.

For the first three centuries after Jesus' birth, the Nativity wasn't officially celebrated. Those who unofficially observed it combined it with Epiphany on January 6th, which is one of the church's earliest established feasts. Some early Christian leaders like Origen (c.185–c.254) opposed a birthday celebration for Jesus, arguing that birthdays were for pagan gods and that only sinners, not saints, celebrated them. But not everyone agreed with Origen, and in time other scholars tried to pinpoint a date for celebrating Christ's birthday. March 25th was an important date in the Middle Ages for the celebration of the Feast of Annunciation, a celebration of Gabriel's visit to Mary to tell her the news that she would carry the Son of God. Over the years more people wanted to celebrate the Nativity itself. And it seemed fitting to count nine months

after the Feast of Annunciation on March
25th to reach December 25th. It was already a
popular date for pagan festivals and fell at the
time of the winter solstice, so church leaders
felt it appropriate to present a new festival
celebrating the Son of the one, true God! The
Middle English Term was *Christemass*, meaning
"Christ Mass," a service of worship for Christ.

Whether December 25th is accurate or not,
what matters is that we do have an official day
on the calendar to celebrate the Savior's birth, a
holiday that people in every nation around the
world celebrate each year. In the United States
Christmas was declared a federal holiday on
June 26, 1870.

SANTA CLAUS

The legend of Santa Claus, the icon of secular Christmas traditions today, is inspired mostly from St. Nicholas of Myra, who was a fourth-century Christian bishop in Asia Minor. He became known as a hero, and many speculated that he possessed supernatural powers—saving lives, healing the sick, and praying powerfully. He was especially known for his wisdom, compassion, and generosity, so much so that, throughout the centuries, he has become the patron saint for many groups of people.

St. Nicholas died on December 6th in the mid-fourth century, but he would not be forgotten by the people who loved him. A traditional feast began each year on December 6th, and on the night before, St. Nicholas's Eve, children put out food for St. Nicholas and straw for his donkey. The next morning, good children would find candy and toys in place of their gifts for St. Nicholas.

A tenth-century Christian writer named Metaphrastes helped keep the history of St. Nicholas alive by collecting stories of his good deeds and inspiring many people to adopt his generosity. Eventually many European countries had created a character resembling St. Nicholas, and over time he merged with their Christmas traditions. In Germany he was *Weinachtsmann* (Christmas man), in France *Pere Noel*, in England Father Christmas, and in the Netherlands *Sinterklaas*. In the early 1800s, American Christmas traditions involving St. Nicholas and gift giving began to take shape, mostly due to the Dutch influence in New York City. The Dutch name Sinterklaas evolved into "Santy Claus" and eventually "Santa Claus."

The look and legend of Santa Claus has evolved a bit since the early nineteenth century with the help of poets and artists, but the importance is still the same: he was a servant of God whose generosity and faith we can believe in.

CHRISTMAS TREES

In America, bringing evergreen trees into homes as Christmas decorations is a tradition that's less than two hundred years old. But its origins are more than one thousand years old. Vikings brought evergreens into their homes as symbols of hope and strength during cold, harsh, often deadly winters. There's a story that in the seventh century, an English Christian monk named Boniface, during one of his missionary trips across Europe, came upon a group of men about to offer a human sacrifice to the Norse god, Thor. Boniface tried to stop the men, and when they refused, he struck the huge oak tree that the men were gathered around. Miraculously the huge oak fell to the ground, and a tiny fir tree could be seen just behind where the oak had stood. Boniface explained that the fir tree that stayed green even in winter represented the eternal life that Christ offered them. He also pointed to the three points of its triangular shape and said that they represented the Holy Trinity of God the Father, the Son, and the Holy Spirit. The story says that the men—who moments before were going to offer a human sacrifice to a pagan god—gave their lives to Jesus Christ at the spot where the evergreen grew.

According to legend, Martin Luther also contributed to the tradition of Christmas trees. The story goes that as he was walking home one December evening in the early 1500s, he was captivated by the starlight shining through the branches of the fir trees. He wanted to re-create the beauty of it, so he tied a candleholder onto a branch of the evergreen in his home. His family and friends were delighted and began adding candles to the evergreens in their own homes. Luther taught that just as the evergreen's color doesn't fade, neither does God's love. And the candlelight was a symbol of the hope Jesus gave to the world through his birth and resurrection.

The Christmas tree was first introduced to the United States during the American Revolution by Hessian mercenaries fighting for the Colonial Army. But the tradition didn't stick then, and it wasn't until Pennsylvania Germans brought the custom in the 1820s that it caught on in the United States.

Nowadays, Christmas trees are decorated in so many ways, often with angels or stars topping them to represent those roles in the Nativity. No matter how they're decorated, their symbolic origin has always been one of hope and strength. And true hope and strength is found in God alone.

CHRISTMAS LIGHTS

Martin Luther is credited for illuminating the first Christmas tree, but those candles tied to evergreen branches were obviously a fire hazard. Despite the amount of house fires and deaths caused by candlelit Christmas trees, people were in love with the beauty of them and didn't want to exclude them from their Christmas traditions, no matter the risk. So in 1882, an employee of Thomas Edison's named Edward Johnson came up with the idea to use the lightbulb that Edison had invented three years before to somehow illuminate Christmas trees. Johnson strung eighty small, colored lightbulbs together and hung them at home on the family Christmas tree. He, his family, his neighbors, and passersby were mesmerized by the beautiful glow coming from the tree, lighting up the room and shining through the window.

But most common people still didn't have electricity in their homes, and the cost of a string of lights like Johnson's was more than one hundred dollars, more than many folks made in a year! But among the wealthy, they did gain popularity, and in 1895 President

Grover Cleveland was proud to claim the first electrically lit Christmas tree in the White House. Within five years, upper-class people everywhere were trying to outdo their neighbors' Christmas lights, spending as much as three thousand dollars per tree.

By the early 1900s, General Electric was producing electric Christmas lights more reasonably priced at twelve dollars a strand. But even those were too costly for the middle class, so they were used most often in department-store displays.

Finally by 1924, General Electric and Westinghouse had created a strand of lights that burned cooler and brighter than ever before—and most importantly were inexpensive enough that nearly everyone could own a set. As electric power lines reached rural America, nearly every average American's Christmas traditions were made more festive with electric lights—spreading the hope of Jesus that Martin Luther believed candlelit Christmas trees represented, but in a much safer way!

MISTLETOE

Even though it's a parasitic plant—mooching life off its hosts, such as apple, poplar, maple, and oak trees—mistletoe has become a symbol of Christmas. Like fir trees, mistletoe is an evergreen plant that does not die during harsh winters, so it has been honored as a symbol of hope, strength, and life since ancient times because of its ability to thrive and flower beautifully in bleak circumstances.

By the Middle Ages, mistletoe was used for all sorts of purposes: Its leaves and berries, while potentially poisonous, were diluted and used in medicines to treat ailments such as epilepsy, tuberculosis, and stroke. Superstitiously it was placed over doors of homes and babies' cribs to ward off illness and evil spirits. And according to legend, mistletoe was the deadliest of weapons and could bring down any warrior instantly. That warrior could only be healed if a loved one used mistletoe berries to restore him.

The legend of the healing power of mistletoe berries traveled to England and became the source of mistletoe as a symbol of love. If a couple passed under mistletoe, they must stop and kiss, and God would bless them with eternal love.

In 1843 Christians adopted mistletoe as a symbol of Christmas, because while mistletoe represented everlasting life to so many, Christ truly brought the hope of eternal life when He came to the world as our Savior. Christians all across Europe soon hung mistletoe to proclaim their enduring faith in Jesus Christ, rather than for superstitious reasons.

Today most think of mistletoe as just a fun holiday decoration and a good reason to kiss a loved one. But there's a much deeper meaning if we think of it as a symbol of the love of Jesus, the eternal life He offers us, and the enduring power of faith in Him.

ADVENT

From the Latin word *adventus*, meaning "coming" or "arrival," the Advent season is a time for preparing spiritually for the coming of Christmas. It was officially established by church leaders in the sixth century to encourage Christians to reflect on the coming of Jesus as a baby, the coming of Jesus into the hearts and lives of those who accept Him as Savior, and the Second Coming of Jesus when He returns in the future.

The Advent wreath was one of the first tangible ways for Christians to remember the season. The Vikings of northern Europe had long brought evergreens into their homes as symbols of hope and strength through the long winters. And Christians of the region would cut branches off the trees and fashion them into Advent wreaths and place a candle on each wreath to represent the light Jesus brought to the world.

As time passed, Advent wreaths became a tradition throughout Europe and more candles were added to symbolize each week of the season. Three of the candles were often purple and represented hope, peace, and love. A fourth candle was commonly red, symbolizing the new life found in Christ because of His sacrifice on the cross. Some added a final white candle, which was lit on Christmas Eve, to represent the birth of Jesus.

During the Middle Ages, stand-alone candles became important in remembering the Advent season. One large candle was marked to represent each day between the Sunday of Advent and Christmas Eve. The candle was lit daily and burned until it reached the next mark. Other traditions included lighting a new candle for each day of Advent. On the final day, with all the candles burning, one large candle was lit and then slowly the others extinguished until the large one representing Christ was the only one left burning.

In some churches, one new candle was lit every Sunday of Advent. The first represented the prophets who foretold the coming of Jesus. The second was for the Bible. The third was for Mary and her acceptance of the role of the mother of Jesus. And on the final Sunday of Advent, the fourth candle was lit and stood for John the Baptist. A larger fifth candle often stood in the middle of the other four and was lit on Christmas Day to represent Jesus.

Today the best-known Advent tradition is the Advent calendar, which originated in Germany, possibly around the turn of the twentieth century. There, families often celebrated with Advent wreaths, but in place of candles, they hung twenty-four small bags on the wreath, one for each day from December 1st to Christmas Eve. Inside each bag was a special treat for children. This concept led to the Advent calendars we know today.

As a German child during Advent, Gerhard Lang was allowed to have one piece of candy per day, which he took off a numbered board his mother had made to represent the days of Advent. As an adult and partner in a printing company, Lang remembered that tradition and created twenty-four tiny pictures to be glued on any large calendar. By 1908 these evolved into calendars that had little doors or windows for children to open and find a little treat such as a candy or toy or decoration. By the end of World War II, these Advent calendars had spread across Europe and the United States and often included scripture and pictures of the Nativity.

CHRISTMAS CARDS

There's no busier time at the post office than the month of December when Christmas cards are sent. And personal mailboxes are busier, too, with the sending and receiving of holiday greetings to and from family and friends. This holiday tradition began in England in 1843. Sir Henry Cole was a very busy high society man, who had multiple jobs as a writer, editor, publisher, and museum director, among others. During the Christmas season, his pile of holiday letters grew so large and overwhelming, he worried that he would never have time to answer them all and would offend the many family, friends, and business associates who'd sent them. One day while working, he folded a heavy piece of paper and thought about a school assignment years before where his teacher had asked her students to draw pictures of what Christmas meant to them.

Inspired with a new idea, Cole met with an artist friend named John Calcott Horsley and commissioned him to illustrate the heavy, folded papers with Christmas scenes—families celebrating around the holiday table and two more scenes to stir the cards' recipients to compassion and generosity during the Christmas season. After the drawings were done, Cole took the card to the printer and had the words *A Merry Christmas and a Happy New Year to You* added. He had one thousand of them printed to answer his holiday mail.

Cole and Horsley's Christmas card was a success and within two years, thousands of English families were sharing their Christmas greetings using Christmas cards. By the mid-1850s, scores of artists and publishers were creating Christmas cards, and the new tradition of commercial Christmas cards was popular in all of Europe.

A German printer named Louis Prang introduced the Christmas card to the United States soon after the Civil War ended and Christmas had begun to be celebrated widely again. With his business savvy in color printing and publishing, he made Christmas cards popular in America and is remembered as the "Father of the American Christmas Card."

Today Christmas cards come in many shapes and sizes and with all kinds of different artwork, some celebrate the Savior, others just celebrate the festive season. But they all originated with a man who wanted to spread Christmas greetings and inspire compassion and generosity in his family and friends.

CANDY CANES

Candy was one of the first special treats given to children as Christmas gifts. A simple, single-color, hard-candy stick or other similar confection was often all it took to delight many children who rarely received such a treat.

While there are many legends associated with the candy cane, church history records support this one from 1670 Germany. At Cologne Cathedral, the choirmaster was trying to figure out how to keep the children in the choir quiet and content during long church services. Rather than punish bad behavior, he wanted to encourage and reward good behavior, and candy was an obvious motivator. He decided on the popular white sticks of candy he knew the children loved, figuring the long-lasting treat would keep them occupied and quiet when they were not singing. The only problem was how to convince priests and parents that children should be allowed to eat candy in church. Brilliantly, the choirmaster realized he could also use the candy as a teaching tool. He asked the candy maker to bend the top of the sticks to resemble a shepherd's staff. That reminder of the shepherds who came to visit baby Jesus along with the white color to represent the sinless life of Jesus would make a lovely symbol for a children's lesson. The congregation and priests of Cologne Cathedral were pleased with the choirmaster's candy lesson, and the children, especially, were happily quiet with their treat during the long Christmas Eve service. Within a hundred years, white candy canes were common decorations for Christmas trees in Germany, and children couldn't wait to take the tree down so they could finally eat them!

Another more ambiguous legend of the candy cane comes from England. A Christian candy maker created a candy cane as a type of signal or code to identify fellow Christians in public during times in England when celebrating Christmas was banned. It's believed these white candy canes also displayed three thin red stripes representing the Father, Son, and Holy Spirit, and a fourth thick red stripe symbolizing the redemptive power of Christ's blood.

Candy canes likely came to America

before the Revolution, but they didn't become a popular decoration and treat for Christmas until after the Civil War. By the early 1900s, they were incredibly popular in America, and in the 1920s they took on the look we know today with a process for hand-twisting colors into the candy cane. In Indiana, a candy maker whose brother was a priest knew the story and symbolism of the red-and-white-striped candy canes from England, so he created candy canes that represented this legend and shared his own faith as well. He used red stripes for the Trinity and power of the blood of Christ, the hook for the shepherd's staff, a background of white to represent the purity of Jesus, and possibly even said that the hook upside down was a *J* for Jesus.

We don't know all the details of the candy cane, but the vague stories we do have make it certain that the candy cane is not just a pretty and tasty holiday decoration. It's a sweet and symbolic representation of the redeeming love of Jesus.

"THE TWELVE DAYS OF CHRISTMAS"

Most people would agree that "The Twelve Days of Christmas" is a rather ridiculous-sounding song! What type of "true love" ever gave gifts like swimming swans and leaping lords to his or her sweetheart? Many people believe that this is just a fun Christmas carol that began as a type of holiday game in the 1700s, but there's a religious legend that suggests a deeper meaning of "The Twelve Days of Christmas."

The story that some argue is pure speculation goes back to the 1500s, when teaching the Catholic faith was illegal in England. The Catholic church went underground, and clerics disguised important elements of their teaching by creating poems that would seem silly to people who didn't know their true meaning. "The Twelve Days of Christmas" is said to be one of those teaching tools.

Contrary to what most people think about the song's title, it doesn't refer to the days leading up to Christmas. Instead it's talking about the twelve days that fall between Christmas and Epiphany on January 6th. Epiphany, which is a celebration of the wise men's discovery of Jesus, is not widely recognized in the United States, but it's very important in other areas of the world such as Europe and Latin America.

The "true love" of the song might not be someone's sweetheart but the Catholic church's code words for God. The recipient of the gifts in the song is said to be anyone who has accepted Jesus Christ as the Son of God and as their personal Savior. And the religious meaning of the twelve gifts?

- A partridge in a pear tree represents Jesus Christ whose birthday is celebrated on the first day of Christmas. A partridge is a bird that will die to protect its young.
- Two turtledoves represent the Old and New Testaments of the Bible.
- Three French hens represent faith, hope, and love, referring to the famous love chapter of the Bible, 1 Corinthians 13.
- Four calling birds represent the four Gospels of Matthew, Mark, Luke, and John.

- Five golden rings represent the first five books of the Old Testament—Genesis, Exodus, Leviticus, Numbers, and Deuteronomy—also known as the Torah or Pentateuch.
- Six geese a-laying represent the six days God used for Creation.
- Seven swans a-swimming represent the seven gifts of the Holy Spirit—prophecy, ministry, teaching, exhortation, giving, leading, and compassion.
- Eight maids a-milking represent how Jesus came to save everyone, even those in lowly positions like milkmaids. The number eight might refer to the beatitudes, where Jesus blessed the poor in spirit, those who mourn, the meek, those who hunger and thirst for righteousness, the merciful, the pure in heart, the peacemakers, and those who are persecuted for righteousness' sake (Matthew 5:3–10).
- Nine ladies dancing represent the fruits of the Spirit—love, joy, peace, patience,

kindness, goodness, faithfulness, gentleness, and self-control (Galatians 5:22–23).

- Ten lords a-leaping represent the Ten Commandments.
- Eleven pipers piping represent Jesus' disciples. Originally there were twelve, but since Judas betrayed Jesus, only eleven spread the Gospel.
- Twelve drummers drumming represent the Twelve Points of doctrine found in the Apostles' Creed.

Whether it's only a fun song or not, if we take time to consider a deeper meaning to "The Twelve Days of Christmas," we find a clever way to remember important basic elements of the Christian faith.

XMAS

Many people find the common tradition of replacing the word *Christmas* with *Xmas* an offensive one. Yes, today it is often done simply to save time or space in writing out the whole word, and many believe it is wrong to take the name of Christ out of the holiday that celebrates His birth. But replacing Jesus Christ's name with *X*, is actually one of the oldest Christian traditions.

Back in New Testament times, many of the first Gentile followers of Jesus were Greek, and their name for Christ was *Xristos* (pronounced Christos). And while symbols of a fish were commonly used to indicate churches and Christian gathering places, the letter *X* (pronounced chi) was also used as a symbol of Christian faith and a marker for Christian churches. When Christians were martyred, other believers often traced an *X* to mark the spot where they had died. During the Dark Ages, *X* was an important symbol for believers who couldn't read or write but could easily remember a simple *X* to represent their faith.

In the 1500s, the word *Xmas* first began to

appear in Catholic writings as more and more European church leaders began to document the history of Christianity. It was used partly to make the word stand out with flair on a page and partly to save on time and resources. Mostly it was used to acknowledge the Greek language and the history of the church and to honor Christ and those who were martyred for Him.

When we see or use *Xmas* today, we can view it not as an exclusion of Christ but as a sign of tribute and love for Him.

There are so many festive ways to celebrate Christmas. Some have deeper meanings and fascinating history, and some really are just for fun. But no matter what traditions we participate in or how we celebrate, we can choose to ponder all our actions and the purposes in our Christmas activities and "do it all for the glory of God" (1 Corinthians 10:31).

Jesus, it's so easy to get caught up in the bustle of the holidays and forget what all this is really for. I believe the whole purpose of this season is to remember You and the gift of hope and salvation You brought to the world. Help me to please You in every tradition I participate in and in everything I do this Christmas and always. Jesus, I believe we should honor You in everything we do!

REFERENCES

The Case for Christmas by Lee Strobel

A Christmas Compendium by J. John

Christmas! Traditions, Celebrations, and Food Across Europe by Stella Ross Collins

Encyclopedia of Christmas by Tanya Gulevich

Joy to the World: The Stories Behind Your Favorite Christmas Carols by Kenneth W. Osbeck

The New Evidence that Demands a Verdict by Josh McDowell

Stories Behind the Great Traditions of Christmas by Ace Collins

Stories Behind the Best-Loved Songs of Christmas by Ace Collins

Why the Nativity? by David Jeremiah